T0063311

Not Broken

Making the Transition to living with Physical Disability

Andrea M. Orsini

BALBOA.
PRESS
A DIVISION OF HAY HOUSE

Balboa Press books may be ordered through booksellers or by contacting:

Balboa Press
A Division of Hay House
1663 Liberty Drive
Bloomington, IN 47403
www.balboapress.com
1 (877) 407-4847

Printed in the United States of America.

ISBN: 978-1-4525-9788-1 (sc)
ISBN: 978-1-4525-9789-8 (e)

Balboa Press rev. date: 2/3/2015

This book is dedicated to a man who
has devoted his life to human rights

"The Bear"

Paul L. Rein

Contents

Acknowledgment

I am grateful to the clients I coached in those first nineteen years. Working with them not only gave me the opportunity to share my ideas with them, but also the opportunity to learn so much from each of them.

Without them my work could not have evolved.

Preface

I created this book because I made every mistake I could possibly make with the onset of my own physical disability. The good news is that I learned from every one of those mistakes. I want to share what I've learned with others who are going through a similar experience. Perhaps your own transition will benefit from this sharing.

The foundation of this book is simple: You can choose points of view that strengthen you or you can choose points of view that weaken you.

This work is made up of practical information and strategies based upon my own experiences and what I have learned as a Challenge Coach. The information is easy to understand and easy to use. I am not a psychologist and this is not a psychological work. In addition to actual strategies

I also offer you my thoughts, ideas, insights and tidbits of information.

Physical disability and I met when I was 40 years old. My own transition to living with physical disability was very rough. I promised myself that if I ever made a successful transition, I would assist others to have a successful transition as well. After I was emotionally on the right track, I began working with people with new physical disabilities. Because I learned by making mistakes, it was important to me to share what I learned with others, so I volunteered my time as a Challenge Coach for nineteen years.

After that I formed a non-profit corporation called Plan B Living, to assist folks to make the transition to living with physical disability through the modalities of workshops and challenge coaching.

I have deliberately kept the information in this book as condensed and to the point as possible so you can begin to use it right away.

This book may inform you of what I did wrong and the ways I corrected those errors, but in reality it is all about your future.

We are all different. No one strategy will work for everyone. The information I present for your consideration is not meant to be a model for your life. Hopefully, by using this information as a framework, you can experiment with the strategies, thoughts or ideas. Then you will learn what does and does not work for you. You will be able to adjust and revise the information in ways that allow you to create your own magic.

Change is Life.
Your response to change determines
the quality of your life.

If change is life, then do you think it might be in your best interest to cultivate changes in your points of view that will enable you to raise the quality of your life?

Our interaction will be based upon exploring alternate points of view that will enhance your ability to negotiate a successful transition to living with physical disability.

The Foundation

When I work with someone this is the formula I use:

There is no blame
There is no judgment
There is no should or must
Whatever you feel is normal for you
We work with what is

It is important for you to extend these same courtesies to yourself. You are allowed to expect these courtesies from others. You are allowed to decide how you want to be treated. You are allowed to decide for yourself the kind of interaction you want. You are allowed to set any boundaries that serve your emotional well being. Maintaining your self-respect is the first step in reclaiming the momentum of your life.

You are not broken unless you choose to believe you are broken. Who you are is determined by what fills your heart, your soul and your spirit. After physical disability, it remains the same. Who you are is still determined by what fills your heart, your soul and your spirit.

Are you willing to deliberately cultivate points of view that allow you to feel this?

The Mistakes

It is important to acknowledge your true self. It is equally important not to allow the viewpoint of another person to undermine you.

Let me share two huge mistakes I made after the onset of my physical disability. I allowed my view of myself to be determined by someone else. I also created phantoms in my view of myself. I did not focus on the facts of my situation. It was because of these mistakes that I spent two whole years of my life without one good thing happening.

While I was still in the hospital, I had questions and concerns. I was wondering if I would have a relationship with my children. I was wondering how I could ever use my Certifications in Firefighting and Heavy Rescue again. I was wondering how I could give up the guitar and piano I loved; the long walks and gardening I loved. I was wondering if I had the guts to follow a new path or even try. Despite those very natural concerns, I had a good outlook. I was hopeful.

When I went home from the hospital I was still pondering those concerns and my outlook was still good. As soon as I got home my husband handed me a loaded pistol, said it was a welcome home gift, and then left the room. My mistake was my point of view of that event. My emotional response at that time of physical and emotional weakness was to internalize and personalize that sad event. It caused a deep conviction that I no longer had value of any kind. My good outlook and hopeful attitude immediately disappeared. Had I been adept at expanding my point of view, I would have realized that it was his weakness, selfishness and insecurity I was witnessing. I would not have taken on the additional emotional burden of believing I had become worthless.

After that event I should have focused my thoughts and all of my attention on my attributes. I should have been appreciating my favorite saying of all time that is brave and forward-thinking.

A ship is safe in harbor:
But that's not what ships are for
Anonymous

- 4 -

Doesn't that saying present a wonderful metaphor for life?

We are not beautiful strong ships designed to remain in one safe spot. We are designed with the resiliency to weather the tempests of our lives. We are designed to be lured and enticed by our dreams and to follow joy to our purpose.

But instead of that brave outlook, I continued my mistake and shut myself off from a connection we must treasure and preserve. I shut myself off from my own potential. Then I set the anchor and began to wither. It would be a long time before I realized what I had done.

The lesson was a painful one. If you should find yourself in a similar situation, I hope you will not allow the weakness and littleness of another person to become yours. Instead, honor yourself. How do you do that? Think of all the things you like about yourself. Think of the things you have done in your life that you are proud of. Remember all the times your attributes have been praised and then honor yourself for every bit of it.

Here are the phantoms I created. It is important to accept only the actual facts of your life changes. I did not. I made assumptions about my situation when my life changes were brand new and my pain was fresh. Foolishly, I also clung to a strong inner resistance to see the actual facts. The facts remain the same even if we do not like them.

The true facts will empower you. When you recognize them your focus will be on your real challenge, not on phantoms of your own creation. The facts of your challenge will be overcome, but those phantoms will forever defeat you.

The Insight

This is how my most important insight was gifted to me. It was the turning point that reconnected me with my potential when all was at its darkest.

While sitting on the porch I saw a neighborhood cat dragging a package of lunch meat back and forth on the sidewalk. She had a plan. She would drag the package for awhile then she would chew on it for awhile. This procedure went on for a very long time, but I continued to watch.

Eventually, the cat succeeded. As I watched her eating, I began to understand what had actually happened. She was able to achieve victory because she accepted the true facts of her situation. That is why she could answer the challenge.

She was hungry. She had food. She had to get the food out of the package to eat it. That was her whole challenge. She did not alter the facts in her mind by creating resistance to achieving her goal. She did not say things to herself to set up her own failure such as, "I've never seen this kind of package before. This kind cannot be opened." The cat was only able to understand her objective of opening the package of lunch meat so she could eat.

Should I change my tactics too and find the true facts of my situation and not alter the facts in my mind? Thankfully my answer was yes. Morph the cat taught me to look at the true facts of my situation and to develop a plan to overcome the obstacles in my path. I remain grateful for this insight.

Where do insights come from? I am certain that life-changing insight was not generated by me. I have grown to believe there is an all-powerful, all-knowing, benevolent Guardian who already provided the tools I need to overcome every challenge before me.

When we lose our way, we are nudged by insights or intuition. All we must do to receive these life gifts is to be receptive to finding them in every experience.

Some of my life lessons are frequently in use. European immigrants taught me to expect good things and to have fun with our differences. A strange old lady taught me we are all alike and all worth loving. Rudolph Nureyev taught me to find the gift in someone's anger. A flood taught me to change loss to blessing. A cup of coffee taught me patience and self-validation.

If you are able to look at every experience with an open mind, your gifts will appear. It is true that sometimes it is difficult to see a gift, even if it is staring at you. I have certainly experienced this.

As an example, I suffered with TMJ for many years. After developing the disease called scleroderma, I experienced a thickening of tissue in front of each ear. Initially, I was so concerned with the appearance of built-up tissue that I did not notice that my jaw was reset and I no longer suffered with TMJ. That was an extremely benevolent gift.

When my house flooded it was a huge blessing. I was able to use the insurance money, not just to repair, but to create a friendly and efficient wheelchair environment. That was another benevolent gift.

My physical disability itself turned out to be another benevolent gift. It got rid of a weak and selfish husband. It took from me everything I had used to earn a living. After my struggles, I found my soul's work in becoming a Challenge Coach. I assure you that nothing makes me happier than when a client informs me they know their strengths and no longer need me!

So how do we become receptive and invite these gifts into our existence? I believe one way is to concentrate on a candle flame. I know this sounds strange, but when you focus on a candle flame and train yourself to notice everything about it: The colors, changing shape, various colors and shadows cast. You are in essence also training yourself to notice everything about your experiences. You are opening your mind to enlarge the scope of your vision. Once you do this, it naturally follows that you will see more than you did before. You will find your life gifts.

Try not to miss a thing about each experience. Practice makes perfect.

TRANSITION STRATEGY

The CareGiver

I don't know the key to success, but the key
to failure is trying to please everybody
Bill Cosby

When we are at our weakest is the time to strive to make the very best decisions for our well being and our future. Yes, it is also the most difficult time to make the best decisions.

When physical disability is sustained, it is also the time to decide how you want to utilize a CareGiver, if one is needed. How much control do you want a CareGiver to have over your life? There is no right or wrong answer. Each individual must act in his own best interest. The point is that whatever you choose to do, be sure to give it sufficient thought so you will have no regrets. Here are a few clarifying questions you can ask yourself.

Do I want to make my own choices and decisions about my life or do I want someone else to make my choices and decisions for me?

Is my goal to learn to do as much for myself as I possibly can, or do I want someone else to do everything for me?

Do I want to utilize my CareGiver as a helpful assistant who can give me the support I need to achieve what is important to me or do I want my CareGiver to take control?

Keep in mind that once you give power over your life to someone else, it is extremely difficult to get it back if you change your mind later.

It is easy to slip into a dependent mental state without even knowing it. I only urge you to give a great deal of thought to this issue so that you make a conscious decision that is truly what you want. After all, it is you who will be living with the results of your decision.

If dependency is your choice, then be content with your decision and I wish you well.

For those of you who want to be as independent as possible, to make your own choices and to reclaim the momentum of your life, you can turn your CareGiver into your cheerleader. Set a goal or intention and ask your CareGiver to assist you to reach your goal by arranging your environment in a way that allows you the best possible advantage to reach your goal. No one can know what you need as well as you do. Think about it and then ask your CareGiver to set up the best arrangement you could think of. When you accomplish your goal, celebrate your achievement and the assistance of your CareGiver. Next, set the new goal or intention and request their valuable assistance again. State your goal often and praise their assistance as well.

One suggestion: Break your goal or intention into small steps. Don't set yourself up for failure by choosing a goal that is too advanced at the present moment.

You are allowed to make any decision that will improve your quality of life. No one but you can know what that means. Go for it.

TRANSITION STRATEGY

Familiarity

Familiarity is a gentle healing medium. Just think about this. When you experience a strong disappointment, at first you cannot get it out of your mind. Then little by little your disappointment becomes familiar and you can accept it calmly.

When you apply this principle of familiarity to physical disability it is a healing medium as well. Remember we talked about the value of seeing the actual facts about your disability? Now let's expand the concept to utilize familiarity to soften the emotional edges of physical disability. Do not be afraid to say your life has changed. If you are honest with yourself about the actual facts of your situation, it will lead to familiarity. Familiarity leads to emotional healing. Emotional healing leads to recognizing your potential.

There is another way to utilize familiarity as well.

There may be times that you feel you have no control over your life. This is a natural occurrence. During those times you can choose everything you are able to.

Rather than listen to the radio, choose a specific CD.

You can choose to select a movie to watch as opposed to just leaving the television on.

You can choose certain clothing or colors to wear that day.

You may have a book you enjoy. During these low points it might be a good idea to choose a familiar and loved book.

You know yourself. Make every familiar choice in your power to get through these low points. They will last a shorter period of time if you make as many personal choices as possible.

TRANSITION STRATEGY

Discovering your Strengths

Knowing others is wisdom. Knowing
the self is enlightenment
Lao-Tzu

*A*t first it was easier for me to recognize loss than it was to recognize strength. After my most important insight I realized that keeping my focus on loss was harmful. If I was focusing on actual facts, then I also had to focus on my assets. So I invented this thinking exercise. For every loss I named, I named five assets. My attention was slowly drawn away from loss to my assets.

When I began to have this productive point of view, I also began to list my assets on paper. I defined my assets as my physical, personal and spiritual gifts, talents, skills and attributes. I must admit that initially my list of assets was not very long, but over time I noticed more and more assets that I possessed.

This exercise taught me that my assets greatly outnumbered my losses.

Notes

My Assets

TRANSITION STRATEGY

Creating New Definitions of Old Words

This strategy assists you to feel good about your efforts. It gives you permission to be gentle with yourself and to remove pressure and stress.

You begin by using key words that identify you in your own mind.

This strategy will serve you more effectively if you identify your personal traits rather than jobs you have done.

It is important for you to feel good about your efforts during transition. Initially there will be activities that are challenging and frustrating. I can promise you that it gets easier as you gain more experience. In the meantime I hope you will not try to meet your past expectations. This is a time to extend love, gentleness and patience toward yourself. Another thought is: Do you place value on what you accomplish or value on how quickly you accomplished it? In our new thinking, it will be more productive to focus on what you accomplish no matter how long it takes. I know this is a new concept for most people, but it was much easier for me to keep my pleasant attitude after I gave up placing value on how long something took me to do. In any case, with practice of the activity itself, you become faster at doing it with just the passing of time. Relax and give yourself a break.

I was always punctual and it was a key self-identity word for me. As an example, you can temporarily redefine punctual as however late you now tend to be until you become proficient with your new methods of getting ready. Then you can return to the old definition of punctual if you choose.

I remember I also temporarily redefined success as getting my clothes on frontward and accomplishing two very small tasks per day. Experiencing success almost every day in this manner was a positive and effective coping strategy during transition.

Be creative. There is no limit. Redefine as many words as you feel are necessary to gain confidence.

All periods of transition in our lives are periods of temporary weakness. Not weakness of mind or character, but weakness because our changes put us off balance. Redefining words will assist you to recognize that you are just temporarily off balance.

Notes

Words I believe identify me

TRANSITION STRATEGY

Confusion to Clarity

If you have experienced confusion or if you sometimes feel you are dull and unresponsive, you may be experiencing an odd after-effect that can occur when physical disability is sustained in mid-life. The feelings are a mixture of confusion, associations that no longer make sense and a feeling that everything is tilted. I call this negative mixture of feelings Spontaneity Shock.

Before you sustained your physical changes, your life had a tone and rhythm that was natural, easy and familiar. The ways you interacted were spontaneous and effortless.

The loss of your natural body language is a major cause of the emotional mixture I call Spontaneity Shock. It is very difficult to recognize that you are no longer using forms of communication that you never even thought about.

I began to become aware when I noticed that people did not respond to me in the ways I had come to expect. I was determined to find out why. Slowly I put the information together, experimented with my own behavior and then realized what had happened. It was difficult to discern because that unconscious level of communication underlines all of our interaction.

I coach many folks with new physical disabilities who are concerned because family members tell them they have a blank look much of the time, or they look confused. I did too. A family member actually told people my mind was gone. He said this right in front of me. Here is a word of warning to every family member out there. We may look dazed or confused, but we understand everything you say.

According to Shyam Bhatawdekar of Building Leadership and Management, "Our communication is made up of 10% words, 30% sounds and 60% body language." Non-verbal language makes up the majority of our communication. That information helps make it easier to understand why there is often the after-effect I call Spontaneity Shock.

To counteract this, you can take inventory of your facial expressions and body movements. Then you can create a brand new non-verbal language for yourself.

TRANSITION STRATEGY

Finding What Was Lost

*If you can change a thought, you
can change the entire scope of your
future to unlimited possibilities*

Some loss is forever, sort of. I suggest you take the time to analyze what components of a prior activity brought you joy. Then keep a sharp lookout for any occurrence that creates those same feelings. As an example, I danced ballet for many years and it was a great personal joy. That exact activity is gone forever, it is true. But the feelings it gave me are not. I had the insight that long road trips gave me the same feelings as ballet. They were feelings that identified me: Satisfaction in my level of self-discipline, satisfaction in my level of endurance and satisfaction in my ability to skillfully move among the other performers. I felt like the real me.

We can experience feelings that identify us by just paying attention to how activities make us feel. In your new thoughts, try to look at the underside of an activity you loved. Why did you love it? What feelings did it give you? Which of your characteristics did it highlight? Which of your attributes did it make you feel proud of? What feelings identify you to yourself?

This insight created a vivid sense of reality for me. I learned that joy is not superficial. It was not just the movement of ballet that I loved. Joy comes from a deep inner level of our being. We experience joy when the attributes we believe identify us are acknowledged and highlighted.

You have not lost your feelings. Try to pay attention to your feelings and allow yourself to feel joy.

Please don't forget that mental activities work the same way as the physical. Pay attention to the feelings your mental activities bring so you can expand those feelings into new ideas. Try to appreciate every level of yourself; every feeling, every mental activity that identifies you to yourself. Our deepest levels are our most meaningful ones.

Notes

Feelings that identify me

TRANSITION STRATEGY

Where is Your Power?

It isn't what we don't know that gives us
trouble, it's what we know that ain't so
Will Rogers

Throughout this book the common theme is the willingness to change points of view.

What if you have everything you will ever need already inside you? I believe you are ready to begin to look at everything from the point of view of your assets.

Your assets are your personal, physical, mental and spiritual gifts, talents, skills and attributes.

There is no obstacle or challenge that can stop you if you are willing to look at everything from the point of view of your assets.

If it is so easy, then why don't all of us do this? Actually, we are stopped. We come to a halt because most of us have unkind self-talk.

Our initial goal is to replace unkind self talk. We may belittle ourselves or think about past discomforts. It takes a deliberate determination to change the natural tendency of unkind self-talk.

The initial goal is to replace unkind or unproductive self-talk with productive and empowering self-talk. It is not complicated. The object is to become accustomed to acknowledging your good efforts and to praise yourself when appropriate. In order to do this, first pay attention to your thoughts. When an unwanted thought creeps into your mind, quickly change it to a thought that will contribute to your sense of well being.

In time you will empower yourself to become so familiar with your assets that you can draw upon just the right asset to overcome the present obstacle.

Please don't forget to turn away from thoughts such as I could achieve that..............if I only had........ if I only could..................if I could only buy, and so on. Instead, focus on what is already in your possession; your assets.

Here is an example from one of my coaching clients. She wanted to clip her fingernails. However, she only had one hand. She did not want anyone else to do it for her. Impossible you say? It is impossible if you only look at the reasons it cannot be done. Finally, she took inventory of what she had: Imagination, legs, feet, arm. Then she saw the solution. She had forgotten about her feet. She placed the nail clipper under a foot, positioned her nail in the clipper and pushed the clipper closed with her foot. Now that is using your assets! She was delighted that she was able to perform this function by herself. It also gave her self-confidence a big boost.

When we look at all of our assets, one can be found that answers the challenge.

Give this a try. You have nothing to lose. I tested this out on myself with interesting results. I diligently changed my unproductive self-talk for six weeks. One day I was placing my purchases in my van and left the ramp down while I positioned everything. Suddenly, I heard a woman laughing. I poked my head out of the van and asked if I could be of assistance. She told me she enjoyed listening to me praise myself. "You were congratulating yourself for finding the best prices and for bypassing items you didn't really need. You also like the way you arranged your purchases in your van so nothing will fall if you must make a hasty stop." I was surprised indeed. I was not aware that I was praising myself out loud. At that time I called my experiment a success. I had reversed unproductive self-talk to recognition and praise of my assets and efforts. I told the woman about my experiment and she asked me to give her a crash course. I did and she left feeling empowered.

Praise your assets and efforts and you can claim victory over obstacles and challenges.

You will not get what you want with what you don't have

TRANSITION STRATEGY

Imagination

You can use your imagination and your broad point of view to achieve.

A very practical application is to:

List tasks you think you cannot do.

Take a good, long look around your home and forget what everything was designed for originally.

Rather, look at everything with a broad point of view. Here is a small but true example from a client. He could not open the screw cap on a soft drink bottle because of limited use of his hands. In order to give his hand better leverage and widen his grip, he uses an old-type metal nut cracker to open bottles.

So get busy and look around your home. The pizza cutter is another useful object. I'll let your imagination work on that.

The dish towel is also a remarkably versatile tool. If you are in a wheelchair, which in essence means that you are shorter than you used to be, you can have folded dish towels placed under things that are too far away and use a reacher to grab the dish towel and pull the object to you, and you will not even scratch the surfaces.

Pretend you are in one of my workshops. I challenge you to come up with fifty ways to use a dish towel.

Have fun with your imagination!

A person with no imagination is a prisoner,
trapped in his own narrow mind
Glen Stephens

Notes

Items in my home that can be used in new ways

TRANSITION STRATEGY

Releasing Your Courage

There may be times when you feel fear. This is very natural. What is important is for you to realize that you do not have to find or develop courage. You already have a great deal of courage. It just needs to be released.

One significant aspect of releasing courage is not to rush it. There is no need for that kind of stress.

If you want, you can practice releasing your courage in small ways until you gain experience. The technique is the same either way.

There are only three steps to release your courage.

First.. Choose your goal. It is important to complete your goals one at a time.

Second. We utilize our old friend, familiarity. Keep thinking about your goal. Think about it as much as you possibly can. Allow those thoughts to saturate you. When thinking about your goal comes automatically to you and when you feel very comfortable with your goal, you can decide to move forward.

Third. Visualize your goal. See yourself in your mind performing your goal. Visualize this over and over again. Then visualize it again and again until you begin to automatically see yourself performing your goal. If your intuition tells you that changes are necessary in the way you see yourself performing your goal, then make the changes in your mind and visualize your goal including the changes. Do this over and over again.

There will come a time when you feel comfortable performing your goal because it feels so familiar to you. All the strangeness will be gone.

Relax and keep watching yourself perform your goal in your mind's eye.

You can reach your goal!

TRANSITION STRATEGY

The Firefighter Mentality

We have already talked about keeping your mind on the goal.

When faced with obstacles, think of yourself as a firefighter. They keep their minds on the goal.

Firefighters have an important mission to perform. They are not deterred by anything as long as they are still functioning.

You will not be deterred from your mission either. Think firefighter and keep moving toward your goal.

TRANSITION STRATEGY

Preparing your Mind

repare your mind to face new challenges each day.

Prepare your mind to keep a good attitude throughout the day...no matter what.

Prepare your mind to embrace and accept your physical pain for one more day.

Prepare your mind to see everything around you with an expanded point of view.

Prepare your mind to perform your daily tasks without pressuring yourself.

Prepare your mind to experience a wonderful day.

I encourage you to begin each day by having conversations with yourself that will give you the best day possible.

Attitude is a little thing that makes
A big difference
Winston Churchill

TRANSITION STRATEGY

Opportunities and Possibilities

*What lies behind us and what lies before us
are small matters compared to what lies within us*
Ralph Waldo Emerson

During our journey together, you may have come to realize that you have control over your thinking. That means you can choose your point of view and you can choose your attitude.

If your point of view is to focus on what you have, then you will begin to see your assets in new and different combinations and to appreciate the expansion of opportunities and possibilities now available to you. Your entire level of understanding becomes more intense and informed. New information that was previously denied you is now part of your life.

You can choose to paint the landscape of your life using a more colorful palette.

During this phase of development, a more tender side of transition begins. Your heart and soul begin to overflow with seeds of possibilities. When you nourish these seeds with self-kindness, self-love and self-respect, they take root and then anything can happen.

Also during the tender side of transition, you may notice a greater appreciation for kindness and consideration. Your own behavior may take on a deeper level of thoughtfulness as well. It is also possible that your spiritual reflexes become more satisfying. Because you feel more deeply, everything of interest to you takes on a more profound dimension and a new idea can grow into a new passion.

These opportunities and possibilities come from keeping your attention on your assets and deliberately choosing broad points of view.

TRANSITION STRATEGY

Not Broken

I believe it is naïveté that may cause the perception of being broken. I suspect it is an offshoot of believing you are less than you were before.

Once you have thoroughly examined how much you have gained in life experience, empathy, understanding, creativity, new goals and imagination, can you really believe you are less than you were before?

I am certain I am much more than I was before. I have a greater understanding and adaptability for new situations, my thinking is expansive and flexible, I have a deeper sense of empathy, a broader perspective of living, the fulfillment of doing my soul's work and deep feelings of gratitude for the insights that make it possible for me to function at a high level despite any disadvantages.

Once your base of knowledge expands and you recognize that all meaningful success in this life comes from inside your thoughts, your points of view and your attitude, breaking is not possible. You are everything that fills your heart and soul and spirit.

You cannot lose if you never give up
Glen Stephens

Best Wishes

I hope you were able to find information that will assist you in making a smooth transition to living with physical disability.

When you have your own insights, I ask that you share them with others. There cannot be too much sharing in this world.

If you wish to contact me about what you have read in this book, you may email me at
amo@planbliving.org

Sincerely,
Andrea M. Orsini

Notes

My own thoughts and ideas about my transition